Investing for Beginners

Minimize Risk, Maximize Returns,
Grow Your Wealth, and Achieve
Financial Freedom Through The Stock
Market, Index Funds, Options Trading,
Cryptocurrency, Real Estate, and More.

Samuel Feron

ISBN: 9781835123010

Contents

.

Introduction

A lthough we have a sneaking notion you know what investing is, let's define some terms first. After that, we'll explain how to proceed.

What is investing? Investing entails making a financial commitment in the hopes of generating a profit. This means you invest money to generate income and meet your financial objectives.

Many people invest their money in the stock market to achieve their long-term financial goals since they can expect a high return. But for new investors in particular, investing can appear frightening and intimidating. Fortunately, many choices are regarded as the best investments for beginners and fit various goals, spending limits, and comfort levels.

If you're just starting, investing may seem overwhelming, but it's essential in growing wealth and saving for various financial goals. Don't become too preoccupied with whether or not now is the best time to begin investing because you will encounter various market settings during your career.

However, before making any investments, new investors must be aware of their risk tolerance. Some investments are riskier than others, so you don't want to get a rude surprise after you've made a purchase. Consider your ability to go without the money you will be investing and whether you can go a few years or longer without having access to them.

No matter where you put your money into investments, you essentially donate it to a business, the government, or another organization hoping they will give you more money. The majority of the time, when people invest money, they have a particular goal in mind, such as retirement, their children's education, a house, and the list goes on.

Trading and saving are not the same as investing. Investing is typically connected with setting money aside for a long time instead of trading stocks regularly. Saving money is safer than investing. Investments are not always assured, but savings are occasionally assured. You would never have more money than you had saved for yourself if you kept your money hidden under your mattress and didn't invest it.

Consequently, a lot of people decide to invest their money. You can make various investments, and this book will cover them all.

Given that you are reading this book, we can assume that you are keen to grasp the basics of investing. The most popular options will be covered in this book, but a financial advisor can also help you choose the best course of action and offer guidance when you make your first investments.

1

Introduction To Investing

To put it simply, investing can help you succeed in life. It may be essential to your ability to develop your worth over time and secure the kind of future you want for your family and yourself. It might even enable you to make money while you sleep. There is no doubt that learning how anything works is worthwhile.

But it's a lot when you're new. Lots of options, unfamiliar terminology and ideas, and challenging, often conflicting counsel to sort through. Additionally, it might be stressful because it involves putting your money on the line.

However, it doesn't necessarily have to be complicated simply because it can be. To begin investing, you only need to make a few key decisions. Let's dissect everything. But first, the basics.

Why Should You Invest?

There are several reasons why investing your money is crucial. You want to make money for future ambitions, help in times of need, job loss, or both. It would help to use compounding while accounting for inflation to prevent your money from losing value over time. Additionally, investment is important to help you reach your goals if you intend to retire and stop working at some point.

Let's look at some factors that make investing so crucial.

Wealth Creation

Wealth may imply different things to various people; It could be a specific sum of money in your bank account or a set of financial objectives you have established for yourself. In either case, investing can help in your progress.

If you aim to pay off debt, put your child through college, purchase a home, launch a business, or save for retirement, investment can help you get there more quickly than just letting money sit in your bank account. Investing can improve your wealth or the worth of all of your assets.

Creating wealth is a long-term goal that will benefit you. You can leave a financial legacy by creating generational wealth through investment. In addition to giving your children a solid financial foundation, passing wealth down to future generations could help close the wealth gap many communities are struggling with.

Compounding

Compound interest can be used to your advantage while investing. Compound interest is the interest you receive on the money you invest plus the interest from each previous period.

Sometimes, it is referred to as "interest on interest." Compound interest enables speedy wealth growth. For instance, your total investment would be $9,000 if you made $50 a month for 15 years. In that period, assuming a 10% rate of return, compound interest would allow the $9,000 to rise to over $19,000.

Reduce Inflation

The general increased tendency in product prices over time is referred to as "inflation". Your money will purchase less today than it did yesterday if prices rise over time. Even though the cost of living has grown, your money will be much less valuable if there is inflation over a 30- or 40-year period. One way to fight inflation is to invest your money. If you earn more than the rate of inflation, your money will be worth more tomorrow than it is today.

Retirement

You must have a sizeable sum of money set aside to support yourself when you stop working if you plan to retire and stop working. The difference between your savings and what you'll need to live on for the next 20 or 30 years can be filled by investing.

Working backward from the retirement savings target you've set for yourself, you can begin investing for retirement. Thinking about your desired retirement date, anticipated retirement lifestyle, and costs will help you reach that figure. You can then develop an investment plan for retirement that balances your present financial condition with your desired retirement lifestyle.

Common Investing Misconceptions And Myths

Because they appear genuine or near the truth, some of the most pervasive myths are challenging to separate from reality. Confused?

Here's an illustration. A mother asked her son if he had finished his schoolwork. "I've finished exercise 2," he said in response. Even though this statement might be true, it doesn't solve the homework completion problem. Even if the son had told his mother the truth, he might still have misled her because this exercise 2 was only a small portion of his schoolwork.

The same is true of convincing investment myths. It is easy to become a victim of financial misconceptions because of many moving components and unforeseen possibilities. Investors are often misled by these myths, misunderstandings, and near-lies, which causes them to make foolish financial decisions.

Therefore, understanding the differences between investment myths and reality is the key to becoming a good investor. We'll outline this section's top seven investing myths so you don't fall for them.

Myth 1 - It Is Too Risky

There are risks associated with investing, yes. Because of this, it is always accompanied by the disclaimer, "You may not get back what you invest."

Yet too perilous? Before you can respond, we must first investigate how risk operates and what it might entail.

A scale of risk can be used to classify all investments. High-risk, volatile investments like hedge betting are at the scale's end. These are not for the timid, as your initial investment's value may fluctuate greatly. This implies that you might profit greatly or possibly lose everything. This kind of investment is not one we recommend.

Some extremely low-risk investments labeled as "cautious" can be found at the sad end of the spectrum. Invest in one of these, and even if there is risk involved, it is unlikely that the value will change much. As a result, you might eventually experience a milder, smoother ride.

There is an investment for every risk appetite, from the conservative to the daring and everything in between. Understanding the risks involved and how they could vary over time is crucial. In this manner, you can decide how much risk is appropriate.

Why even take a risk? In short, it could provide your money with more growth potential than cash savings.

Myth 2 - You Have To Be Rich

Despite the fact that it used to be the case, you can now begin investing with less money than you might anticipate. And it's now easier than ever thanks to smartphone applications, online fund platforms, and online investing advice services.

You can start investing online or using our mobile banking app with a one-time contribution of £50 if you have an eligible or active savings account. There are further prerequisites for eligibility.

There is a 0.25 percent quarterly yearly account charge as well as ongoing fees equal to 0.25 percent of the value of your investments.

Before you apply, you will have access to the breakdown of these expenses.

Myth 3 - You Must Lock Up Your Cash

It's likely that you've encountered phrases like "You should aim to hold it for at least five years" or "An investment should be seen as a medium to long-term commitment." This is due to the fact that the likelihood that snags will be smoothed out increases the longer you hold onto an investment.

This does not imply that you must physically lock away your money. Most investments don't lock up your money or charge fees when you sell your investments. You always have access to your money.

An investment shouldn't be viewed the same way as a savings account. Early withdrawals could have a detrimental impact on your results. Avoid being compelled to sell during a market collapse since your investments can be worth less than you invested.

Before investing, you should set aside three to six months' expenses in an emergency fund. Therefore, you can utilize your money to fix your automobile if it breaks down while the markets are in uproar. In this manner, you can let your assets grow while giving the markets time to stabilize.

Myth 4 - You Must Be A Professional

You must research and monitor the markets if you decide to invest in shares. This is due to the possibility of a financial loss if the firm in which you invest performs poorly. The overall state of the economy, interest rates, and supply and demand will all impact the price of your shares.

But purchasing shares isn't the only investment option. Funds may be a smart place to start if you're new to investing. Purchasing a fund is similar to purchasing a ready-made investment basket. They disperse your funds over numerous investments, equivalent to putting all your eggs in a basket.

Investing in funds rather than individual shares of a single company can reduce risk. This is so that a higher return on another could offset a lower return on one investment. This method of risk distribution is referred to as "diversification."

The fact that funds are put together by a fund manager, an expert financial professional, is arguably the best part about investing in them. Essentially, you are paying a professional to make investments on your behalf. The charges paid to the fund manager are taken directly out of the investment.

Myth 5 - You Should Keep An Eye On Your Investments Every Day

Keeping a close eye on the markets? Most likely, you have better things to do with your time. This is yet another factor that makes pre-built portfolios a viable investment option. They are expertly managed to ensure they remain at the level of risk you specify. You can make an investment with a pre-made portfolio and then essentially set it and forget it. To check on its progress, you only have to sneak a peek now and then.

Even if you invest in shares and adopt a hands-on strategy, you don't necessarily need to track them daily. The majority of online share trading providers provide features to help with this. By setting up share price notifications, your phone will ring whenever a stock rises above or below a specified level.

Myth 6 - You Must Understand When To Make A Purchase

There is a belief that to profit from the markets, one must buy stocks when they are cheap and sell them at a profit. Investors might need much time and effort to determine when a share price has peaked or bottomed out.

But there are a lot of things that affect the stock market. Results are essentially impossible to predict. Both crucial are starting as soon as possible and continuing your investments for as long as possible. There will be some downturns and possibly some difficult years, but if you're not compelled to sell during a downturn (see myth 3), you might be able to weather any storm.

Consider your investment horizon before making a decision. More volatility can be manageable if your timeframe is longer because you will have more time to bounce back from any lows.

For instance, you would want to make a conservative investment if you have five years till retirement. You might be able to be more daring if you had at least ten years to play with. Once more, if you're unsure what's best for you, you can ask a financial expert for their advice. Fees and eligibility requirements apply.

Myth 7 - It's An Easy Way To Get Rich

Influencers on social media may claim it's easy to profit from risky trades. But don't fall for it. Consider what transpired during the Dotcom bubble in the late 1990s and what has happened with cryptocurrencies over the past several years.

In general, markets favor long-term investors. It would help to have discipline, patience, and a cool, calm head instead of passion to allow your investments to flourish.

2

Building A Strong Financial Foundation

You're not alone if setting financial priorities seems like an intimidating task. Quite a few people put off managing their money because they don't know where to begin: Should I get life insurance or maximize my retirement savings? Which should I prioritize: saving for a home or my child's college fund?

Financial tasks can be divided into smaller, more manageable segments to help with planning. As you create a financial road map for you and your family, consider the following.

Set Financial Goals You Can Keep

The financial goal involves any strategy you have for managing your money. You can set short-term and long-term financial goals, such as saving $1,000 or investing for retirement. Every area of your life should have goals, but clear financial objectives enable you to put your money where your mouth is.

Additionally, I cannot discuss financial goals without mentioning the Baby Steps. Making financial decisions can be as challenging as deciding what to watch on Netflix. There are so many choices, and everyone has a preference.

Do you need to pay off debt? Do you put money aside for your children's college? Buying a home? Investing for the future? Your road to completing all those tasks is apparent in the 7 Baby Steps, which cut through the chaos. It helps you concentrate on one goal at a time to achieve more progress with your money and enjoy the financial calm. So, if you don't know how to set financial goals, keep the following in mind.

Try To Avoid Setting Too Ambitious Goals

It may be easy to feel as though you must achieve all of your financial objectives at once, such as maxing out your retirement contributions, fully repaying your debts, and cutting back on your discretionary spending to boost your savings. However, if you set goals that are probably beyond of your current reach, you can feel let down if you don't reach them.

The 'All or nothing' mentality is one of the difficulties in setting goals. It's an extreme viewpoint, and when we act in that way, we leave ourselves open to failure because we don't take into account all the gray areas in life. It won't be easy to check your budget and ensure you have an extra $500 each month if you aim to save $500 but haven't even begun saving $50 a month.

Even if your goals seem small, like saving $50 per month, doing so will help you develop sound money management skills you can maintain over the long run. You can feel driven to move on to bigger goals by accomplishing your present goals.

Concentrate On Bringing Forth Progressive Changes

Focusing on goals that allow you room to develop over time will help you avoid setting too aggressive ones. One tactic is to commit to doing something like, "I'm going to increase my savings by 1%, and every few months, I'll review my budget and increase my savings by another 1%." More unsustainable than doing the opposite is going from saving nothing to saving a significant sum of money.

Additionally, it's important to remember that things might change. You could spend more money in some months than others because of notable occasions like holidays, birthdays, and weddings. Your spending might be a little less in some months. Because of this, it's crucial to extend yourself some mercy and begin by making small, beneficial changes to how you spend your money. Additionally, when your income and budget rise over time, you might have additional room to advance even further toward your long-term goals.

Recognize That Unexpected Financial Occurrences Will Always Happen

It might seem great to progress toward any financial objective, such as paying off credit card debt until you need to use your credit card again in an emergency, and the pay-off cycle begins again. Even when you've accomplished a major goal, managing your money still involves a lot of emotion since you could feel additional pressure to keep it up. When it seems like there are always fresh expenses slipping up on you, that might be challenging to achieve.

With money, there's always this unforeseen circumstance that arises. It becomes easier the sooner we accept that as a fact. Perhaps your car breaks down, or you receive a surprise bill. It would help if you incorporated this into your financial plan to avoid being caught off guard and to prevent your progress from being halted.

Starting an emergency fund is one approach to being ready for unforeseen costs. You can utilize the money in your emergency fund, which is a separate savings account, to pay for any unforeseen expenses. By doing so, you can cover that unexpected payment or an urgent car repair without incurring too much debt.

Financial professionals often advise putting emergency funds into high-yield savings accounts, enabling you to earn more monthly interest than conventional banks. In this method, even if you aren't making regular donations, your money will still increase faster.

Determine What Is Most Practicable For You Using Your Budget

Knowing your expenses and spending patterns is the final and possibly most important piece of advice for creating realistic financial objectives. Then, you can make goals that are suitable for your circumstances.

Tracking your expenses and charges may not be particularly comforting, especially if you've never done it before. It's possible that you'll decide to concentrate on this financial goal in 2024 if you've never before made a monthly spending plan.

Other strategies include looking over your bank statements and compiling a list of your monthly expenses. As an alternative, you may use a budgeting application like Mint or Empower (formerly Personal Capital), which can connect to your bank accounts, investment accounts, and other financial accounts. Your transactions will be tracked by an automated budgeting tool, which will classify them so you can see what you spend the most money on overall.

After that, you can deliberate on where to reduce (or even increase) your expenditure and how to distribute money to reach your new objectives.

The Power Of Saving And Compound Interest

Compound interest is your best friend, and time is your most precious asset when investing. You've come to the right place if you recently started your first job or are beginning a side hustle but are unsure what that "compound interest" term in the last line means.

You're in a terrific position as a young person to start having your money work for you. Why? Since growth quickens with time and you still have a long way to go, saving now will pay off greatly in the long run. Here is all the information you need about compound interest and how to use it to your advantage.

<u>What Is Compound Interest?</u>

Simple interest must first be understood to understand compound interest. Simple interest solely refers to the interest you receive on your savings. Consider that you want to invest $100. This is your principal balance. You visit the bank and deposit the money into a savings account that offers 1% interest. This means that after having your $100 primary balance in savings for one period (usually a year), you will have earned $1, or 1%, on your investment. Since this keeps happening every year, you will receive another 1%, or $1, the next year, and so on. That is simple interest.

Contrarily, compound interest allows your wealth to increase more quickly throughout your life by paying interest on your principal balance and interest accrued over time. Do you recall studying exponents in school? A related idea is compound interest.

Let's return to the first $100. Imagine making a 1% annual compound interest deposit of the same amount into a bank. How does that develop differently from a simple interest rate? Well, it doesn't after the first year. You will still have earned $1 more than your principal balance. But instead of your initial deposit, that $100 principal balance, you will start earning 1% interest on your new account balance of $101 the following year. You earn $1.01 on the amount rather than $1, increasing your account balance to $102.01. That $102,01 gains 1% interest the following year, growing to $103,03. This keeps compounding, or growing, increasing how much you make the following year, the year after, and so forth.

How Does Compound Interest Work?

Compound interest grows ever-increasingly since it includes all prior interest that has accrued. The amount of compounding periods or years you have been saving makes a big difference, so you should start investing as soon as possible.

You will increase if you deposit money into a compound interest-earning account and leave it there. In the preceding illustration, you made a $100 investment and let compound interest take care of the rest. However, if you were to consistently add more money to your principal account balance (for example, every quarter, month, or pay period), your money could truly start to start working for you.

Of course, when you're young and beginning from scratch with your finances, it isn't easy to picture saving money consistently. But doing so has a genuine advantage. From a young age, investing a small sum every month, even just $100, has the potential to grow into a sizable sum of money you can depend on when it's time to retire.

How Does Compound Interest Actually Appear In The Real World?

Real-world compound interest will look different based on your rate of return, where you invest your money, and how much you save.

Consider the following illustration:

Investor One, Charlie, began saving when he was 25. He saved $1,000 monthly for ten years, up until age 35. He stopped saving after that, but he kept his money in his investment account, which continued to grow at a 1.5% rate until he retired at age 65.

Investor Two, Molly, began saving when she was 35. Also, she saved $1,000 monthly for ten years until she was 45. She did the same as Charlie and kept the money in her investment account, which grew at a 1.5% rate until she was 65.

Max, the third investor, started investing at age 45. Like others, he saved $1,000 per month for ten years before stopping his savings at age 55 and letting his money grow at a 1.5% rate until he was 65.

For ten years, each of the three investors put the same amount, $120,000, into their savings. But when they started saving, their retirement outcomes were very different. In the end, Charlie had $203,105 in savings, compared to Molly's $174,831 and Max's $150,492.

Simply put: Compound interest works best when you invest your money early.

Which Investing Strategy Is Best For Me?

What should you do with your money now? Compound interest profits may grow even more quickly if you invest in a tax-advantaged retirement account or aren't taxed on the money until you withdraw it in retirement. If you're a full-time employee, the simplest place to start is by making contributions to your employer's 401(k), a popular tax-advantaged retirement savings account. You'll have the chance to begin saving for the future as you get older through retirement accounts like IRAs and Roth IRAs. But for now, it could make more sense to talk to an adult in your life about the various savings accounts accessible to you if all you're doing is babysitting after school or working as a lifeguard on Saturdays at the pool.

Wintrust can help in this situation. Young investors can access excellent account options from Wintrust, your top community bank, and financial education tools and resources. Wintrust can assist you if you have questions about what is best for you. Through a savings plan suitable for your particular needs, their advisors can assist you in achieving your goals. Connect with a local Wintrust banker to position yourself for the future.

3

Getting Started
With Stocks

W hen you buy stocks, you bet on the company's
long-term success and growth. One of the best ways
for novices to learn how to invest in stocks is by making a
deposit into an online investment account that can then be
used to buy shares of stock or stock mutual funds.

For the price of one share of stock, you can start investing by
opening a brokerage account. Some brokers also provide pa-
per trading, enabling you to practice trading stocks using stock
market simulators before making a real-money investment.

Exploring Different Types Of Stocks

Historically, stock market investing is one of the key routes to
financial success. When researching stocks, you'll often hear
them described in various stock categories and classifications.
These are the main stock types that you need to be aware of.

Preferred Stock And Common Stock

Common stock makes up the majority of stock investments. Shareholders of common stock, representing a component of a company's ownership, are entitled to a proportionate share of the assets' value if the business is dissolved. Shareholders of common stock have theoretically limitless upside potential; however, they also risk losing everything if the business fails with no assets left over.

Differently, preferred stock grants owners the right to get a specific amount of money back in case of a firm dissolution before common shareholders. Additionally, preferred shareholders are entitled to dividend distributions ahead of common shareholders. Overall, this leads to preferred stock having more in common with fixed-income bond investments than standard common stock as an investment. A corporation will often only sell common stock. This makes sense because stockholders typically want to acquire that.

Large-Cap, Mid-Cap, And Small-Cap Stocks

The market capitalization of stocks refers to how much money their shares collectively are worth. The largest market capitalizations of firms are called large-cap stocks, while successively smaller companies are represented by mid-cap and small-cap stocks.

These groups are not well delineated from one another. However, one frequently-used criterion states that equities are considered to be large-cap if their market cap is $10 billion or over, mid-cap if their market cap is between $2 - $10 billion, and small-cap if their market capitalization is under $2 billion.

Mid-cap and small-cap stocks offer higher potential for future growth but are riskier than large-cap equities, typically considered safer and more conservative investments. But just because two businesses are grouped here doesn't indicate they are similar investments or will perform similarly in the future.

Domestic And Foreign Stock Markets

Stocks can be grouped according to their location. Most investors consider the location of the company's official headquarters to help them distinguish domestic U.S. equities from foreign companies.

It's crucial to realize that a stock's geographical classification does not always correlate to the region from which the company derives its sales. A classic example is Philip Morris International (PM 0.34%), which has its headquarters in the United States but sells all its cigarettes and other products completely abroad. It can be challenging to determine a company's true domestic or international status based on business operations and financial data, especially for large multinational businesses.

Value Stocks And Growth Stocks

Another categorization technique distinguishes two common investment strategies. Growth investors typically search for businesses whose sales and profitability are rising quickly. Value investors seek out businesses whose stock is undervalued, whether compared to their rivals or historical stock price.

Growth stocks often carry higher levels of risk, but the potential rewards can be very alluring. Businesses with high and rising customer demand, particularly concerning longer-term societal changes that encourage using their products and services, are successful growth stocks. However, competition can be severe, and if competitors undermine a growth stock's operations, it may swiftly lose popularity. Investors' concern that long-term growth potential is dwindling can often cause even a slight slowdown in growth to cause prices to drop quickly.

Value stocks, however, are thought to be more cautious purchases. They are often established, well-known businesses that have already developed into market leaders and don't have as much room to grow. However, they can be ideal options for people looking for more price stability while still obtaining some of the benefits of exposure to equities because they have dependable business structures that have withstood the test of time.

IPO Stocks

IPO stocks refer to shares of businesses that have just completed an initial public offering. When a new company goes public, investors who want to invest early in a good business idea are often quite excited. However, they can also be risky, particularly if the investment community is divided over their potential for development and profit. After going public, a stock typically keeps its status as an IPO for at least a year and up to two to four years.

Stocks With And Without Dividends

A lot of stocks regularly pay dividends to their shareholders. Because dividends offer significant income to investors, dividend stocks are highly prized in several financial spheres. A corporation qualifies as a dividend stock if it pays even $0.01 per share.

However, stocks are exempt from dividend obligations. Stocks that don't pay dividends can make solid investments if their prices increase. Even if the trend in recent years has been toward more stocks paying dividend payouts to their shareholders, some of the largest corporations in the world still do not pay dividends.

Income Stocks

Since most companies give out income in dividends, income stocks are simply another name for dividend stocks. However, shares of businesses with more established business models and relatively fewer long-term growth potential are also called income stocks. Income stocks are popular among individuals in or close to retirement since they are best for conservative investors who want to withdraw cash from their investment portfolios immediately.

Non-Cyclical And Cyclical Stocks

National economies often experience expansionary and contractionary cycles, boom times, and busts. Investors refer to certain companies as cyclical stocks because they are more vulnerable to general business cycles.

Shares in businesses engaged in manufacturing, travel, and luxury products are examples of cyclical equities because a downturn in the economy might impair consumers' capacity to make large purchases swiftly. However, when economies are strong, a surge in demand may cause these businesses to recover quickly.

Non-cyclical companies, usually called secular or defensive stocks, don't experience those significant fluctuations in demand. Grocery store companies are an example of non-cyclical equities since people still need to eat whether the economy is doing well or poorly. While cyclical stocks often thrive during strong bull markets, non-cyclical stocks typically do better during market downturns.

Safe Stocks

Safe stocks have share prices that fluctuate less than the entire stock market on an up-and-down basis. Safe companies, sometimes referred to as low-volatility equities, typically operate in sectors of the economy that are less subject to shifting economic conditions. Additionally, they often provide dividends, and this revenue can be used to counteract declining share values in trying times.

Sector-Specific Stock

Stocks are often categorized according to the industry they are in. Stock market sectors are among the main classifications that are most frequently used:

- **Communication -** Internet, media, telephone, and leisure service providers

- **Consumer Discretionary -** Retailers, automakers, hotel and restaurant chains, and other businesses

- **Consumer Staples -** Food, beverage, tobacco, household, and personal product manufacturers.

- **Energy -** Firms engaged in the discovery and production of oil and gas, pipeline suppliers, and owners of gas stations

- **Financial Institutions** - Banks, mortgage lenders, insurance providers, and brokerage firms.

- **Healthcare** - Medical device manufacturers, medicine and biotech firms, and health insurance

- **Industrial** - Railroad, aviation, construction, logistics, aerospace, and defense firms

- **Materials** - Mining, forestry, building supplies, packaging, and chemical firms

- **Real Estate** - Firms that maintain and develop properties as well as real estate investment trusts

- **Technology** - Firms that provide hardware, software, semiconductors, communications gear, and IT services

- **Utilities** - Electric, natural gas, water, renewable energy, and multi-product utility corporations.

ESG Stocks

ESG investing is an investment philosophy emphasizing environmental, societal, and governance issues. ESG principles consider additional collateral effects on the environment, business employees, customers, and shareholder rights rather than concentrating solely on whether a firm makes a profit and increases its income over time.

Socially responsible investing, or SRI, is linked to the regulations that govern ESG. SRI investors eliminate equities from businesses that don't align with their core beliefs. ESG investing has a more advantageous aspect, though, in that it actively promotes investing in the companies that perform things the best rather than simply rejecting those that fail important tests. The topic is very interesting because research has shown that adhering to ESG principles can increase investment returns.

Blue Chip Stocks

There are stock categories as well, which make decisions based on perceived quality. Blue Chip firms are often the best of the best in the corporate world, dominating their respective industries and building solid reputations. Although they normally don't offer the maximum profits possible, investors with lesser risk tolerance choose them because of their consistency.

How To Invest In Stock

Investing is a tried-and-true approach to making money work for you as you try to make more money. Warren Buffett, a famous investor, characterized investing as "forgoing consumption now to have the ability to consume more later."

You can increase your money several times if you constantly invest your money. Because of this, it's crucial to start investing as soon as you have any money set aside for the purpose. Furthermore, a fantastic place to start is the stock market.

You can begin whether you have $1,000 saved or can simply afford an extra $25 per week. Remember that there is a lot you can and should learn about stock investing if you want to succeed financially for the time being; read on for the procedure to start the process.

Establish Your Level Of Risk Tolerance

What is your risk tolerance, or how willing are you to take the potential of losing money if you invest? Stocks can be divided into several categories, including value stocks, aggressive growth stocks, high capitalization stocks, and small-cap stocks. There are varying degrees of risk with each. You can focus your investment efforts on the stocks that complement your risk tolerance once you've established it.

Choose Your Investment Goals

Determine your investment goals as well. An online broker like Charles Schwab or Fidelity will ask you about your investing goals and the previously mentioned degree of risk that you're willing to take when you open a brokerage account. An investment goal can be increasing the amount of money in your account if you're just starting your profession. You might desire to make money and build and safeguard your wealth if you're older.

Your investment goals can be to save for college, buy a house, or support your retirement. Goals might evolve. Just be careful to identify them and revisit them occasionally so you can stay focused on accomplishing them.

Choose An Investing Strategy

While some investors like to set and forget it, others desire to manage their money actively. Though your choice could vary, choose a strategy to get going. You could manage your investments and portfolio independently if you are confident in your knowledge and abilities in the field. You can invest in bonds, stocks, exchange-traded funds (ETFs), index funds, and mutual funds using traditional Internet brokers like the two described above.

You can get assistance from a seasoned broker or financial advisor with your investment choices, portfolio management, and portfolio adjustments. This is a wonderful choice for beginners who recognize the value of investing yet may desire the assistance of a professional. An automated, hands-off alternative to working with a broker or financial advisor, robo-advisors are often less expensive. Your goals, level of risk tolerance, and other information are collected by a robo-advisor program, which then automatically invests for you.

Select A Trading Account

Workplace Retirement Plan

If your workplace has a retirement plan like a 401(k), you may invest via it in various stock and bond mutual funds and target-date funds. It might also provide the chance to purchase employer stock.

After enrolling in a plan, you automatically contribute at the specified level. On your behalf, employers could make matching donations. Your account balance grows tax-deferred, and your donations are tax-deductible. This is an excellent approach to increasing your investment returns with little work. Additionally, it can teach investors the discipline of consistent investing.

A Brokerage's Taxable Or IRA Account

Besides having a workplace plan, you can start investing in stocks by creating an individual retirement account. Alternatively, you could choose a standard, taxable brokerage account. You typically have a wide range of stock investment possibilities. Individual stocks, stock mutual funds, exchange-traded funds (ETFs), and stock options may be among them.

An Account With A Robo-Advisor

As previously mentioned, an account of this kind builds a stock portfolio for you according to your investment goals.

Become More Diverse To Lower Your Risk

Understanding diversification in investments is crucial. Simply said, investing in various assets, or diversification, lowers the risk that the performance of one investment will materially impede the return on your entire investment portfolio. It could be interpreted as slang for avoiding putting all your money eggs in one basket.

Diversification might be challenging if your budget is tight when investing in individual equities. For instance, you might only be able to invest in one or two businesses with just $1,000. There is a higher risk as a result.

Mutual funds and ETFs can be useful in this situation. Both types of funds often hold most stocks and other investments. As a result, they offer greater diversification than a single stock.

4

The World Of
Index Funds

I nvestors' concerns about the ability of fund managers to produce the best returns on their mutual fund investments are driving them to choose passively managed products, such as index funds more and more. Before you contemplate investing in index funds, this chapter will provide you with all the information you need about them.

What Is An Index Fund, And How Does It Work?

An index fund is a mutual fund that invests in stocks that closely resemble those in a specific market index. This suggests that the scheme's performance will be consistent with the benchmark index it monitors.

An index is a collection of securities that characterizes a specific market sector. Index funds are considered passive fund management since they follow a certain index. The traded securities in a passively managed fund are based on the underlying benchmark. Additionally, passively managed funds do not need a professional group of research specialists to spot opportunities and select the best stock.

An index fund is created to replicate the performance of its index, as opposed to an actively managed fund that works more and harder to time and outperforms the market. As a result, the returns of index funds match those of the underlying market index.

Except for a little variation known as tracking error, the returns are roughly equivalent to the benchmark. The fund management often makes an effort to minimize this inaccuracy.

Advantages Of Buying Index Funds

The following are some benefits that index funds enjoy:

Low Costs

An effective staff of research analysts is unnecessary to help fund managers select the best companies because an index fund mirrors its underlying benchmark. Additionally, there is no active stock trading. All of these elements result in an index fund's minimized managing costs.

Unbiased Investment

Index funds invest via an automated, law-based process. The fund manager's mandate specifies the amount to be invested in index funds of different securities. By doing this, human judgment or prejudice in making investment decisions is eliminated.

Widespread Exposure

To guarantee that the portfolio is spread across all stocks and industries, investments should be made in a ratio similar to that of an index. An investor can therefore utilize a single index fund to collect the probable returns on the larger market sector. If you invest in a Nifty index fund, you can access 50 securities distributed over 13 industries, from pharmaceuticals to financial services.

Tax Advantages Of Index Fund Investing

Index funds often have a minimum turnover or few trades made by a fund manager in a given year due to their passive management. Less trading results in fewer capital gains and dividends being paid to unitholders.

Easier To Control

Index funds are easier to manage since fund managers don't have to stress about how the market treats the stocks that comprise the index. All a fund manager needs to do is periodically rebalance the portfolio.

Who Should Invest In Index Funds?

When choosing mutual funds, your investing horizon, goals, and risk tolerance should all be considered. Risk-averse investors should use index mutual funds. Such funds don't need in-depth investigation and tracking. For instance, you can choose a Sensex or Nifty index fund if you want to invest in stocks but do not want to expose yourself to the risks of actively managed equity funds.

What Things Should You Consider As An Investor?

Before choosing to invest in index funds, you should think about the factors listed below:

Returns On Index Funds

Index funds seek to match the market index's performance. They do not strive to outperform actively managed funds' benchmarks. Due to tracking issues, the returns generated could occasionally fall short of those of the underlying index. The index fund will perform better the lower the errors are.

Risk-Taking

Index funds are less vulnerable to risks and volatility associated with equities because they represent a specific market index. It makes sense to invest in index funds to get the best returns during a market upswing. However, because index funds often lose value during a slump, things might become ugly. Therefore, a mix of actively and passively managed index funds in your portfolio is always advisable.

Investment Costs

The expense ratio for index funds is naturally 0 less than actively managed funds. The fund manager is not required to develop an investment strategy for index funds. Even a fund with a lower expense ratio should be remembered that it has the potential to produce larger returns on investment.

The Taxing

Redeeming the units of your index fund investment results in capital gains, which are taxed. The holding period, or time you remain invested, determines the taxes rate. Gains with a holding period of up to one year are termed short-term capital gains (STCG) and are subject to a 15% tax (plus any relevant surcharge and 4% health and education). Suppose the total long-term capital gains amount from equity-oriented mutual funds/equity shares exceeds 1,00,000 in a year. In that case, long-term capital gains (LTCG) from funds held for more than 12 months can lead to long-term capital gains tax at 10% (plus surcharge where applicable plus 4% Health & education.)

Investment Time Frame

Index funds are subject to large changes quickly. If these variations persist for a long time, they might even out the returns on your investment. Therefore, index funds are the best choice for investors with a lengthy time horizon. If you choose to buy index funds, you must have the patience to wait for the fund to reach its full performance potential.

How To Invest In Index Funds

An index fund adheres to a market index, which is often made up of stocks or bonds. Typically, index funds invest in every element that makes up the index they follow, and they have fund managers whose job is to ensure that the index fund performs identically to the index.

Choose An Index

With the use of index funds, you can follow countless different indexes. The S&P 500 index has 500 of the best businesses on the American stock market and is the most well-known. Here is a list of a few more prominent indexes, organized by the market segment they cover:

- **Bonds** - Bloomberg Barclays Global Aggregate Bond

- **International Stocks** - MSCI Emerging Markets, MSCI EAFE

- **Small U.S. Stocks** - S&P SmallCap 600, Russell 2000

- **Large U.S. Stocks** - Dow Jones Industrial Average, S&P 500, Nasdaq Composite

In addition to these broad indexes, sector and country indexes focus on stocks in particular industries, style indexes highlight fast-growing businesses or undervalued stocks, and other indexes restrict investment based on their filtering mechanisms.

Pick The Appropriate Fund For Your Index

You can typically locate at least one index fund that follows your chosen index. You may have a dozen options for tracking well-known indexes like the S&P 500. Ask some fundamental questions if you have more than one index fund option for your selected index. First, which index fund, first, closely mirrors the index's performance? Second, which index fund has the lowest fees? Third, can you invest in an index fund despite its restrictions or limitations? Finally, are any further index funds offered by the fund provider that you'd want to use? Choosing the ideal index fund for you should be made easier by the answers to those questions.

Get Shares Of Index Funds

You can register a brokerage account to buy and sell the index fund shares you want. On the other hand, you can open an account directly with the mutual fund provider.

Once more, it pays to consider features and expenses when determining how to purchase index fund shares. Registering a fund account directly through the index fund firm is less expensive because some brokers charge extra for their clients to purchase shares of index funds. However, many investors hold their interests in a single brokerage account. The brokerage option may be your best option to consolidate all your investments under a single account if you want to invest in various index funds offered by various fund managers.

Free Goodwill

Hello there, and thank you so much for joining me as we explore the fascinating world of investing for beginners. We've gone through several key ideas and strategies together, and I hope you feel more prepared to take charge of your financial future now.

I now want to ask you for a small favor that could significantly matter. What you say in response to this book could mean all the difference to someone else who is just beginning their investment career.

Imagine someone intrigued and ready to learn, just like you were not so long ago, but who may also feel overwhelmed or unsure where to start. Your review can be the light they need to follow, giving them the assurance and motivation they require to make that vital first move.

You don't need to be an authority to voice your opinion. Your sincere feedback about how this book benefited you, what you liked best, or any useful advice you learned along the way will go a long way in helping others in making wise choices.

Therefore, if you have time to spare, **I would highly appreciate it if you could leave an honest review.** A few sentences discussing your experience and how it affected your understanding of investment will suffice; it doesn't have to be extensive or complicated. Someone reading your thoughts might find the motivation they require to start their path to financial independence.

Keep in mind that we are all involved in this. By sharing your knowledge, you join a community of people who encourage and help one another achieve their financial goals.

I can't express my gratitude to you enough for taking the time, being committed, and wanting to help others through your review. Your contribution is incredibly important and greatly valued.

Happy investing!

5

Navigating The Options Market

C ontracts known as options grant the buyer the right, however, not the obligation, to buy or sell the asset at a particular price on a particular date. They are called derivatives because the underlying assets give them their value. Trading options is strategy traders employ to speculate, generate income, and reduce risk.

Despite its daunting appearance, options trading delivers substantial gains that cannot be achieved solely by trading shares and ETFs. Trading options involves making predictions movement of the market or share price. Before understanding how to trade options, let's understand how options trading works.

How Does Options Trading Work?

In options trading, traders can purchase a call option if they are bullish about the market and a put option if they wish to wager on dropping prices. Traders who purchase call options set a price at which they will purchase the shares later. In contrast, traders who purchase a put option will decide the price at which they will sell the shares later.

Trading options is a cheap technique to predict an asset's market or share price. This is because traders will have the right but not the obligation to fulfill the contract as a buyer of a call or put option. Traders may decide not to exercise their rights if the contract is not profitable on the expiration day. They would only lose out on the premium in this scenario.

To bet on the markets growing or decreasing and promptly pocket the premium money, traders can also sell the call or put option. However, they must uphold their end of the bargain when they sell.

Traders can purchase both call and put options to profit immediately. Each possible combination of buying and selling possibilities is a strategy.

Types Of Options Trading Strategies

Every trader needs to be familiar with the options trading strategy listed below.

- **Bull Call Spread -** is a bullish technique where the trader purchases one call option and then sells another with a higher strike price. He has a bullish outlook on the market and stands to gain if the price of the underlying securities increases.

- **Bull Put Spread -** In this strategy, the trader will buy a put option and sell a different put option with a higher strike price. When the value of the underlying security rises, the trader will profit.

- **Protective Put Vs. Synthetic Call** - In a synthetic call, the trader purchases both the underlying asset and a put option. If the asset price increases, earnings are infinite; if it decreases, losses are only as great as the premium paid for the put option.

- **Bear Call Spread** - This bearish trading method entails purchasing one call option and selling another with a lower strike price. Profits are only realized when the asset's price declines. Both the earnings and losses in this technique are constrained.

- **Bear Put Spread** - When traders anticipate a slight decline in the markets, they buy a put option and sell a different option with a lower strike price. Profits and losses are constrained. Profits result from a decline in asset price.

- **Protective Call Vs. Synthetic Put** - When the markets decline, the trader benefits from a synthetic put or protective call. This approach combines purchasing a call option while holding a future short position. When the price drops, the profit is limitless, and the loss is only as great as the premium.

- **Long And Short Straddle** - A market-neutral trading strategy known as a long and short straddle combines call and put options with the same strike price. A long straddle offers limitless rewards and no risk. A short straddle, in contrast, offers infinite loss, and rewards are restricted to the premium collected.

- **Long And Short Strangles -** In a long strangle, the trader will purchase a call option with a greater strike price than a put option. Profits are limitless, and losses are only as great as the premium paid. Selling a call with a greater strike price than the put is known as a short strangle. The loss is limitless, and the profit is only as much as the premium.

- **Long And Short Butterfly -** A long and short strategy that combines bullish and bearish spreads while capping gains and losses at a certain amount. It is a balanced strategy with set risks and profits that are capped.

Advantages Of Trading Options

- **Excellent Hedging Tools -** Options are effective hedging tools, but one must utilize them properly. Using options, traders can lower their equity downside risk. For instance, if a trader owns shares in a firm and is concerned that the price will decline, they can purchase a put option to reduce the risk of a decline.

- **Cost-Effective -** Because options are contracts for underlying assets and do not represent ownership, they are less expensive than stocks. For instance, a trader would need to invest $10,000 to buy 100 company shares with a $100 share price. However, they can purchase a contract for 100 shares of options for just $500. Traders can make significant profits on their bets by using the remaining funds as they see fit.

- **Short-Term Potential For Higher Returns -** Options provide a greater potential for short-term superior returns than equities. The trader must, however, employ the appropriate strategies. The profit percentage is larger in options because traders spend less money using options and make earnings practically identical to those made in equities.

The Disadvantages Of Trading Options

Trading options include three decisions: direction, time, and price, which can make it very difficult. Before implementing an option strategy, traders must consider all three factors.

- **Uncertainty Of Gains** - Gains are uncertain because all options strategies are based on assumptions and future expectations. Only when the share prices move in the direction, the trader forecasted will the trader profit. Losses are likely if this does not happen.

- **Trading Commissions And Fees** - Compared to trading in equities, options trading entails hefty trading charges and costs. The costs rise as the strategy becomes more complicated and includes more calls and puts.

- **Tax** - Because all gains from trading options are short-term, they are subject to the 15% short-term capital gains tax. As a result, the trader loses some of the gains to taxes.

Things To Keep In Mind When Trading Options

- **Losses** - When trading options, a small margin is invested, less than the money required to purchase the shares. This can cause traders to lose sight of the size of their potential losses if the market doesn't move in their favor.

- **Liquidity** - Having an exit strategy is essential when trading options. Trade just the options that have a lot of liquidity. Otherwise, there is a risk that funds would freeze and that there will be losses. Although a cheap choice may seem appealing, it is often less liquid than a costly one. Therefore, it's crucial to balance profitability, accessibility, and liquidity.

- **Hedging** - At first, options trading might be very perplexing. To reduce risk and better understand how options work, beginners must combine options with a standard trade. It is preferable to use options for hedging purposes first. It should ideally only be used by seasoned traders to speculate and profit.

Option strategies are most important when traders wish to hedge, speculate, or profit. Making money and reducing risk both require employing the appropriate method.

How To Trade Options

The basic steps in the trading of options are listed below.

Your Goal Should Be Decided

Whatever your trading goal, you'll need a brokerage account authorized to trade options to proceed with any option strategy. Your exact degree of options approval will also affect the trades you can make.

Find Options And Ideas

What other qualities of an option or underlying security are you seeking now that you've determined your main goal? The universe of trades can be reduced to a manageable number of possibilities by filtering the field based on price, volume, implied volatility, sector, or other criteria.

Compare And Analyze Ideas

It's time to contrast your options and trade ideas when you've found a few. Start by evaluating each option's possible risks and rewards and how its price may be influenced by variables, including changes in the underlying stock price, days till expiration, various strike prices and expiration dates, and implied volatility.

Put In A Trade For Options

Have you decided which option to trade? The next step is to place an online order to build your option position. Enter the relevant option order information (type, expiration, strike price, number of contracts, etc.) after selecting the underlying symbol. Your order will be sent to the market when it has been submitted.

Controlling Your Position

Once your options position has been established (opened), it is advisable to monitor it to determine what to do as expiration draws closer by looking at its value and trend.

If you purchased an option, you may sell it before it expires, exercise it, buy or sell the underlying securities, or let the option expire worthless, depending on the underlying asset's price.

You have two options if you sold an option: either buy it back to close the position or let it expire worthless. Additionally, you can be forced to take assignments if you purchase or sell the underlying security.

6

The Rise Of Cryptocurrencies

O ver the past few years, cryptocurrencies have grown in popularity; as of 2018, there were more than 1,600 of them! Additionally, the number keeps rising. As a result, there is a rise in demand for blockchain developers, who create software that powers cryptocurrencies like Bitcoin. Blockchain developers are highly regarded, as evidenced by their wages: a full-stack developer makes an average income of more than $112,000, according to Indeed. Even a dedicated website for cryptocurrency jobs exists.

Whether you're interested in a job as a blockchain developer or just want to stay up to date with the current developments in technology, here we will explain what cryptocurrency is and why it's important and get you off to a good start.

What Is Cryptocurrency?

A cryptocurrency is a coded string of information representing a unit of exchange. Blockchains are peer-to-peer networks that act as secure transaction ledgers while keeping track of and organizing Bitcoin transactions like transferring, buying, and selling. Using encryption technology, cryptocurrencies can act as both money and an accounting system.

A cryptocurrency is a type of virtual or digital money used as a means of transaction. It is very similar to real money, except that it uses encryption instead of having a tangible form.

Since no central bank or body controls how cryptocurrencies operate, additional units can only be introduced if certain requirements are satisfied. For instance, fresh bitcoins can only be created with Bitcoin when a block is uploaded to the blockchain; at this point, the miner is paid in bitcoins. After the 21 millionth bitcoin is created, no more will be made.

How Does Cryptocurrency Work?

Cryptocurrency is a virtual/digital currency that utilizes cryptography for security. This security feature makes cryptocurrencies challenging to counterfeit. Since they are decentralized, cryptocurrencies are not controlled by any one organization, such as the state or financial institutions.

Additionally, distributed ledger technology—typically a blockchain—which serves as a public database of financial transactions—allows for the decentralized control of each coin.

In 2009, the cryptocurrency known as Bitcoin was developed. The process of creating a cryptocurrency is called mining. This involves using computing power to solve difficult mathemathical puzzles that validate transactions on the blockchain, the open ledger of all cryptocurrency transactions. And in exchange for their work, miners receive cryptocurrency.

Trading cryptocurrencies are complex and speculative, and there are big risks involved. Prices are subject to change at any time. Only select investors should invest in cryptocurrencies due to their price volatility. As a result, investing in cryptocurrencies should be regarded as high risk. Know the risks associated with investing before deciding, and seek financial advice.

Benefits Of Cryptocurrency

The cost of a cryptocurrency transaction is negligible or nonexistent, as opposed to, for instance, the cost of sending money from a digital wallet to a bank account. Transactions are not time-limited and are unrestricted for both purchases and withdrawals. Additionally, unlike opening a bank account, anyone can use cryptocurrencies, which necessitates papers and other documentation.

International cryptocurrency transactions are even faster than wire transfers; wire transfers take almost a day to move money between locations. Cryptocurrency transactions are finished in a few minutes or even seconds.

How To Buy Cryptocurrency?

As said earlier, cryptography is used by cryptocurrencies to protect their transactions and control the production of new units. Cryptocurrencies are digital or virtual tokens. And "fiat" money, or conventional currencies like US dollars or euros, is often used to purchase cryptocurrencies. However, cryptocurrencies like Bitcoin or Ethereum can also be used to pay for them. You must initiate a digital wallet to save your funds to purchase cryptocurrencies. Then, you can purchase coins on a cryptocurrency exchange using your fiat money or another cryptocurrency.

There are several options for purchasing cryptocurrencies.

To purchase Bitcoin with a credit/debit card, bank transfer, or other payment method, utilize an online cryptocurrency exchange like Coinbase, Binance, or Kraken.

You can buy cryptocurrencies directly from other users through a peer-to-peer exchange like LocalBitcoins or Bisq.

Using cryptocurrency trading platforms, you may exchange cryptocurrencies for different assets, like stocks.

How To Store Cryptocurrency?

Investing in cryptocurrencies requires secure cryptocurrency storage. There are various ways to store cryptocurrency, but a digital wallet is the most popular. Software-based, web-based, or hardware-based digital wallets are all possible.

Web-based wallets are accessed using a web browser, but software-based wallets must be installed on a computer or mobile device.

A physical device that stores cryptocurrency offline is a hardware-based wallet.

Cryptocurrency is kept, sent, and received using digital wallets. They are generally less vulnerable to malware and hacking than other wallets. However, digital wallets can be recovered or stolen if not properly protected.

To protect the wallet, utilizing two-factor authentication and strong passwords is crucial. Additionally, avoiding address reuse and other security problems can be achieved by utilizing an address produced by a secure random number generator. Additionally, it is best to keep your private key, which has access to your cryptocurrency, confidential.

How To Invest Safely In Cryptocurrency

Before investing in cryptocurrencies, conducting market research and understanding the industry is essential. Recognizing the technologies, advantages, and risks of investing in cryptocurrencies.

- **Use Reputed Exchange Platforms -** Investors should only buy and sell cryptocurrencies on reputable exchanges. Reputable exchange platforms have safety features to shield investors from fraud and theft.

- **Store Cryptocurrency Securely -** After obtaining cryptocurrency, it is essential to store it safely. Investing in a secure wallet is one of the greatest methods to safeguard cryptocurrency against theft and fraud.

- **Diversification -** Investment diversification can help reduce the risks of making Bitcoin investments. For instance, disperse the threat by purchasing many cryptocurrency types.

7

Investing In Real Estate

Although high interest rates might deter investors from buying real estate, they are predicted to flood the market again once rates start to decline. In a recent Bankrate research, 29% of Americans said they would put their money in real estate if they knew they wouldn't need it for at least ten years.

Beyond becoming a landlord, a well-established option for those who prefer to manage a property personally, consumers have various options for investing in real estate. The ability to invest in real estate without having tens of thousands or more in cash is also made easier than ever before by new business platforms.

Benefits Of Real Estate Investing

One of the most popular and profitable investments, real estate has a lot of success potential when done properly. One advantage of real estate investing is a steady income stream that could potentially result in financial independence.

Passive Income Generation Is Possible

You can produce passive income that is almost tax-free by investing in real estate. Even while sleeping, your rental properties will continue to earn you money. You can spend less time working and more time doing what you enjoy if you invest in several rental properties that bring in enough money to pay your expenditures.

It Can Provide Retirement Cash Flow

When done properly, real estate investing is a great way to build wealth over time. Generating income flow for retirement is one of the numerous advantages of real estate investing. This means you might use the money from your rental properties to supplement your retirement income.

Hedge Against Inflation

Real estate investors do not share the dread of inflation that most people do. Property investment is a great way to protect against inflation. Your property's rental income and the value of your investment both increase when the price level does. Thus, the short-term and long-term effects of inflation are shielded from real estate investors.

Real Estate Is A Stable Investment With Ongoing Income

Real estate investments do not vary drastically daily, like investments in the stock market. It is a reliable investment that generates revenue for you. You only periodically collect your ongoing income (also known as Cash-on-Cash Return) to sell when the price has significantly risen, and the market is strong.

You Can Help Others By Having A Home

The satisfaction of giving someone else a home is an under-appreciated advantage of real estate investing, particularly in residential real estate. Everyone needs a place to live, but not everyone has the money upfront to buy a house, leaving renting their only choice. We often hear stories about landlords neglecting their duties and providing certain renters with nightmare-like living situations. Investment in residential real estate guarantees that a family is housed in safe, healthy, clean, and equal conditions in addition to assisting with housing necessities.

For Investors, Real Estate Investing Offers A Variety Of Alternatives

You have the option of investing in single-family homes, multi-family homes, vacant land, and commercial buildings, depending on your initial startup finances, leverage, and preferences. Even if you lack experience, you can start investing in real estate as soon as you have the funds or resources to purchase a home.

Longer Leases Are An Advantage Of Investing In Commercial Real Estate

This is because they can give you more stability and dependability. This is so that they may stay in one place for longer, which is what most businesses desire to do. Real estate is never worthless.

Aside from the fact that real estate values often increase, your investment in real estate can never lose value, even in trying times. We think that if you own a home, you can always sell it. Unlike stocks, real estate never loses value, even when its value declines.

Real Estate Investment Reduces Risk

One of the main pros of using real estate in one's financial portfolio is risk minimization. Yes, having a steady monthly paycheck is a huge benefit, but protection against riskier investments like stocks is often crucial.

Real estate investing has many benefits and is a great method to earn passive income. Due to the increased demand for houses, real estate values often rise, increasing your chances of success. Real estate investing has other significant advantages besides financial ones. See the benefits of real estate investing to understand why this will make a fantastic addition to your portfolio.

Investing In Real Estate In 2023

The increase in interest rates has had a significant impact on the housing market. Because rising rates make homes less affordable for borrowers, owners may need to drop their asking prices to sell a property, as they did for most of 2022 and the beginning of 2023.

Interest rates were still relatively low at the beginning of 2022. Mortgage rates were considerably higher than in 2021, but the Federal Reserve had not yet swiftly raised interest rates. However, the central bank had clarified that it was preparing to raise rates considerably in the coming months. Smart buyers, therefore, sought to lock in reduced mortgage rates on their real estate acquisitions.

The Fed then began raising interest rates at an unprecedented rate. Real estate has become less accessible due to the rate rises, and many property sellers have decreased prices. The average 30-year mortgage rate was just under 7 percent in early 2023, a record high.

But individuals considering getting involved should remember that real estate investing is often a long-term endeavor. Even if interest rates are high now, it might be best to start saving money for a down payment while awaiting a rate decrease.

In light of that, here are the top five strategies to invest in real estate.

1. Purchase Your Own Home

While you would not typically consider your first home an investment, many others do. It provides several advantages and is among the greatest options for investing in real estate.

Your monthly payments can be used to build equity in your property rather than paying rent, which always seems to increase yearly. Some of the monthly mortgage payments you make go into your pocket. However, there is still disagreement among experts regarding the advantages and disadvantages of homeownership, and as homebuyers in the 2000s learned, a house is never a prudent investment.

If you want to live there for an extended period of time, buying a home can make sense because you'll be able to lock in a monthly payment that may be comparable to what you would pay in rent. Additionally, banks provide borrowers with a cheaper mortgage rate and lower down payment requirements for owner-occupied residences, showing them more favorably. Interest costs may also be deductible from your taxes.

2. Make An Investment In A House To Rent Out

You may try renting out a duplex or a single-family home as a residential property if you're ready to take things a step further. The fact that you are aware with the needs of the market makes this sort of property superior to commercial properties like retail centers.

A single-family home can be a good place to start small and with little investment. For a home property, you might buy it for $20,000 or $30,000 instead of the hundreds of thousands required to buy a commercial property. If you can locate a desirable distressed property through foreclosure, you might be able to purchase it even more affordable.

You'll need to put down a sizeable sum as a down payment, often as much as 30% of the purchase price. Therefore, it can be prohibitive if you're just starting and don't have a sizable bankroll yet. It could be possible to get around this by purchasing a rental home where you also reside.

Another drawback is that you'll have to manage the property and decide, for example, what needs upgrading. Even while owning property is viewed as a passive occupation for tax purposes, being a landlord may make it anything but that. Additionally, even if a tenant skips a payment, you must continue making monthly installments to avoid defaulting on the loan.

3. Consider House Flipping

House flipping has grown in popularity but demands a good sense of value and more operational know-how than being a long-term landlord. If you follow this route properly, you could make money more quickly than if you were a landlord.

The major benefit of using this strategy is that you can make money more quickly than simply managing your property, but it also requires more experience. House flippers typically identify undervalued homes needing repairs or a complete renovation. The difference between their all-in pricing (buy price, rehab costs, etc.) and the sales price is what they profit from after making the necessary repairs and charging market value for the homes.

House flippers require a keen eye for what can be mended affordably and what cannot. A house's potential future value must also be estimated. If they make a mistake, their profit could disappear fast or, worse yet, become a complete loss. If a house doesn't sell immediately, the house flipper may be stuck paying interest on the loan until a buyer is found.

4. Purchase A REIT

The next two real estate investment strategies are passive, contrasting the earlier choices. REITs (Real estate investment trusts) are a perfect choice for investors who desire real estate profits with liquidity and ease of stock ownership. Additionally, you are entitled to a dividend.

Compared to conventional real estate investing, REITs offer several benefits and could simplify the process considerably.

However, purchasing REITs has drawbacks of its own. A REIT's price may change when the market swings, just like the price of any stock. As a result, REIT prices could decrease along with the market. This is less of an issue for long-term investors who can weather a downturn, but if you need to sell your stock, you cannot get what it's worth right now.

You must thoroughly analyze any REIT equities you intend to purchase using methods appropriate for a professional analyst. However, purchasing a REIT fund, which owns a variety of REITs and thus diversifies your exposure to any one business or industry, is one method to avoid this drawback.

With a little money, investing in a REIT is a fantastic place to start, but you'll need to put in some effort since there are still some ways to lose money on a REIT investment.

5. Use A Real Estate Website

You may get into real estate on larger commercial ventures using an online real estates platform like Fundrise or Crowd-street without investing hundreds of thousands or even millions of dollars. These platforms assist in bringing together investors and developers eager to finance real estate and profit from potentially pretty lucrative profits.

The main benefit for investors in this situation is the possibility of participating in a rich venture they might not otherwise have been able to access. Depending on the deal's details, investors may be able to participate in either debt or equity investments. These investments could generate returns unrelated to the economy and cash payments, allowing investors to spread their exposure to market-based assets across their portfolios.

However, there are several drawbacks to these sites. Some may not even be useful if you don't already have money because they may only accept accredited investors (such as those with a net worth of $1 million or more). However, while some platforms could demand a minimum investment of $25,000, others can get you in with just $500.

The platforms also levy an annual administration fee, commonly 1 percent, and they may tack on additional charges. That can seem expensive in a world where mutual funds and ETFs can build diverse portfolios of stocks and bonds for as little as 0% commission.

While platforms may screen their investments, you will also need to do so, which calls for the ability to examine the opportunity. The investments often have low liquidity and offer few opportunities for redemption until a particular project is finished. And unlike investments in a REIT or your rental property, you might need to locate another contract once a deal is finished and your investment is repaid to keep your portfolio expanding.

8

Managing Risk In Your Investment Portfolio

F inancially, a risk is the possibility that a result or investment won't produce the desired results or return. Risk
implies the possibility of losing the entire initial investment
or a portion of it.

Risk is typically quantified by taking past actions and results
into account. Standard deviation is a common metric used
to measure risk in finance. The standard deviation calculates
how volatile asset prices are with their average historical values over a specific period.

Understanding the fundamentals of risk and how it is quantified makes it possible and smart to control investment risks.
All types of investors and business managers can prevent
unnecessary and expensive losses by becoming aware of the

risks that can apply to various scenarios and some of the holistic management techniques for managing them.

The Principles Of Risk

Everyone faces everyday risks, whether driving, crossing the street, investing, capital planning, or other activities. The most important variables for individual risk management and investment management are an investor's personality, lifestyle, and age. Their risk profile determines each investor's willingness and resilience to risk. Investors typically anticipate bigger profits to make up for increased investment risk.

The link between risk and return is a cornerstone concept in finance. The potential return increases with the level of risk an investor is willing to accept. Investors must be paid for taking on greater risks because risks can manifest in many ways. For instance, a corporate bond offers a lesser rate of return than a U.S. Treasury bond, which is one of the safest investments. Compared to the US government, a corporation is significantly more likely to file for bankruptcy. Investors are given a greater rate of return on corporate bonds due to the higher default risk.

As said earlier, risk is typically quantified by taking past actions and results into account. Standard deviation is a common metric used to measure risk in finance. A value's standard deviation can be used to gauge its volatility with its historical mean. A high standard deviation denotes a high degree of risk and a high degree of value fluctuation.

To help manage risks related to their investments and business operations, people, financial advisers, and businesses can all adopt risk management plans. Several theories, metrics, and management techniques have been found in the academic world to measure, assess, and manage risks. Standard deviation, beta, Value at Risk (VaR), and the Capital Asset Pricing Model (CAPM) are a few of them. Investors, traders, and business managers can often reduce some risks by utilizing various strategies, such as diversification and derivative positions, after measuring and quantifying the risk.

Riskless Securities

No investment can be completely risk-free, but some assets have so little actual risk that they are considered risk-free or riskless.

Riskless securities often form a baseline for risk analysis and risk measurement. These investment options provide an anticipated rate of return with minimal or no risk. All types of investors often turn to these securities to retain funds that must be promptly available or preserve emergency savings.

CDs, government money market accounts, and US Treasury notes are risk-free investments and securities. Generally speaking, the baseline, risk-free security for financial modeling is a 30-day U.S. Treasury bill. Given its relatively short maturity date and full faith and credit of the US government, it has little interest rate vulnerability.

Risk And Time Horizons

Investments' time horizons and liquidity often influence risk assessment and risk management. Investors who require their money to be available immediately are more inclined to put their money in risk-free securities and are less likely to invest in high-risk or investments that can't be immediately liquidated.

Time horizons will also be crucial to any investor's investing portfolio. Younger investors may be more likely to invest in greater-risk assets with larger potential rewards if they have longer time horizons till retirement. Due to their increased need for funds, older investors would have different risk tolerance.

Types Of Financial Risk

Every investing and saving decision carry a unique set of risks and rewards. Investment risks that impact asset values are often divided into two categories by financial theory: systematic risk and unsystematic risk. Investors are, generally speaking, exposed to both systematic and unsystematic risks.

Systematic risks, usually referred to as market risks, are risks that could have an impact on the majority of the market or the entire economy. Market risk is the possibility of losing money on investments because of political and macroeconomic risks that impact the market's performance. It is difficult to reduce market risk through portfolio diversification. Interest rate risk, inflation risk, currency risk, liquidity risk, nation risk, and sociopolitical risk are some additional prevalent categories of systematic risk.

Unsystematic risk, usually referred to as specific or idiosyncratic risk, solely impacts one sector of the economy or specific business. The risk of losing money on an investment because of a company- or industry-specific risk is known as unsystematic risk. Examples include a product recall, a change in management, a change in regulations that could hurt a company's sales, and the entry of a new competitor with the potential to steal market share from an existing firm.

Diversification is a strategy investors use to control unsystematic risk by investing in various assets. There are various other categories of risk in addition to the general systematic and unsystematic risks, including:

Business Risk

The basic viability of a business—the question of whether a firm can make enough sales and earn enough income to cover its operating costs and turn a profit—is referred to as business risk. Business risk concerns all the additional costs a business must pay to continue operating and functioning, whereas financial risk concerns financing costs.

Salaries, production costs, facility rent, office, and administrative charges are some of these costs. The cost of goods, profit margins, competition, and the overall level of demand for the goods or services a firm provides all impact the organization's business risk.

A business risk known as operational risk can be related to system failures, human error, fraud, or other internal operations that could negatively affect a company's financial performance. Operational risks can be controlled by implementing efficient internal controls, procedures, and systems.

Businesses and investments may be subject to legal risks resulting from amendments to the law, new rules, or court cases. Legal and regulatory risks can be addressed through compliance programs, keeping an eye on changes to rules, and getting legal counsel as necessary.

Default Or Credit Risk

Credit/default risk is the likelihood that a borrower won't be able to fulfill its loan commitments, including paying the contractual interest or principal.

Bond investors are particularly concerned about this risk because they own bonds in their portfolios. The last level of default risk and hence the lowest returns are associated with government bonds, particularly those issued by the federal government. On the other hand, corporate bonds typically have the largest default risk and the highest interest rates.

Investment-grade bonds have a low probability of default, whereas high-yield or trash bonds have a larger probability. Bond rating organizations like Standard and Poor's, Fitch, and Moody's can be used by investors to distinguish between investment-grade and trash bonds.

Country Risk

Country risk is the possibility that a nation won't be able to fulfill its financial obligations. All other financial instruments in a country and other nations with which it has relations can perform poorly when that country defaults on its debts. Stocks, bonds, mutual funds, options, and futures issued in a certain nation are subject to country risk. The countries with the biggest deficits or emerging markets are more likely to experience this risk.

Exchange Rate Risk

When making investments in other countries, one must take currency exchange rates into account because they might influence how much an asset is worth. Foreign exchange risk (exchange rate risk) is a risk that applies to any financial instruments that are denominated in a currency other than your home currency.

For instance, even if you live in the United States and buy in a Canadian stock with Canadian dollars, you could still lose money if the value of the Canadian dollar declines relative to the value of the American dollar.

Interest Rate Risk

Interest rate risk refers to the potential for a change in an investment's value as a result of altering the yield curve's shape, changing the absolute amount of interest rates, the difference between two rates, or any other relationship between interest rates. This type of risk, which has a more direct impact on bond values than stock prices, poses a significant danger to all bondholders. On the secondary market, bond prices are falling as interest rates climb.

Reinvestment risk is linked to interest rate risk. There is a possibility that an investor won't be able to reinvested the cash flows from an investment at the same rate of return as the initial investment, such as interest or dividends. Reinvestment risk is crucial for fixed-income investments like bonds since they are vulnerable to trends in changing interest rates. Investors can reduce reinvestment risk by diversifying their portfolios, laddering their investments, or choosing various maturity dates.

Political Risk

Political risk is the possibility that the profits of an investment could be negatively impacted by political unrest or changes in a nation. This risk may result from a shift in the executive branch, the legislature, other foreign policy decision-makers, or military command. The risk, also called geopolitical risk, increases in importance as an investment's time horizon lengthens.

Counterparty Risk

Counterparty risk is the possibility or likelihood that one of the parties to a transaction could breach a legal commitment. Credit, investment, and trading transactions may be subject to counterparty risk, particularly if they take place in over-the-counter (OTC) marketplaces. Counterparty risk is present in financial investment products such as stocks, options, bonds, and derivatives.

Liquidity Risk

The liquidity risk relates to an investor's capacity to sell their investment for cash. Investors typically demand a premium for illiquid assets to make up for the time they have had to keep securities that are difficult to sell.

Model Risk

This risk results from using financial models to assess risks, price financial instruments, or make investment decisions. Model risk can appear if the model is founded on false premises, flawed information, or flawed techniques, which could result in inaccurate projections and unfavorable financial repercussions. Model risk can be controlled by regularly evaluating and analyzing financial models and employing several models to cross-check results and projections.

Risk VS. Reward

The risk-return tradeoff balances the desire for the lowest risk and the best profits. Generally speaking, high levels of risk are linked to high potential returns, while low levels of risk are linked to low potential returns. Each investor must determine the level of risk they are prepared and able to take in exchange for the desired return. Based on variables including age, income, investment objectives, liquidity requirements, time horizon, and personality.

It's crucial to remember that increased risk doesn't always translate into bigger rewards. The risk-return tradeoff suggests that investments with larger risks may result in better profits, but it makes no guarantees. The risk-free rate of return, or potential rate of return on a risk-free investment, is on the lower end of the risk spectrum. It represents the rate of interest you might anticipate from a completely risk-free investment over a certain time frame. Theoretically, you should anticipate receiving the risk-free rate of return as the minimal return on any investment because you wouldn't take on further risk unless the possible rate of return were higher.

Risk And Diversification

Diversification is the most basic—and efficient—method of reducing risk. The principles of correlation and risk are important to the diversification process. A well-diversified portfolio will include a variety of securities from various industries with variable levels of risk and return correlation.

Diversification is the most crucial factor in assisting an investor in achieving long-term financial goals while reducing risk, even though most investing specialists concur that it cannot guarantee against a loss.

Planning and ensuring proper diversification can be done in several ways, including:

- **Diversify The Investment Vehicles In Your Portfolio** - Such as cash, bonds, mutual funds, ETFs, equities, and other types of funds. Look for investments whose returns historically haven't fluctuated in the same way or to the same extent. Thus, even if a portion of your portfolio loses value, the rest can still increase.

- **Keep Your Investments Diverse Within Each Category** - Include securities that differ according to market capitalization, geography, industry, and sector. Combining several types, such as growth, income, and value, is also smart. Bonds should also take into account various maturities and credit characteristics.

- **Include Securities With Different Risk Levels** - There is no requirement that you choose solely blue-chip stocks. In actuality, the reverse is true. Selecting assets with various rates of return will ensure that significant gains balance out losses in other areas.

Keep in mind that diversifying your portfolio is a continuous process. Businesses and investors do routine "check-ups" or rebalancing to ensure that the degree of risk in their portfolios is consistent with their financial strategy and goals.

Can Portfolio Diversification Offer Risk Protection?

Portfolio diversification is a useful tactic for controlling unsystematic risks (risks related to particular businesses or industries), but it is unable to guard against systematic risks (risks that have an impact on the whole market or a significant portion of it). Diversification cannot eliminate systematic risks like interest rates, inflation, and currency risks. However, by considering additional strategies like hedging, investing in assets that are less linked with the systematic risks, or modifying the investment time horizon, investors can still lessen the impact of these risks.

How Do Risk-Taking And Investment Decisions Differ Depending On Investor Psychology?

Risk-taking and investment decisions are significantly influenced by investor psychology. Investment decisions made by individual investors may be influenced by their perceptions of risk, past experiences, cognitive biases, and emotional responses. For instance, loss aversion is a cognitive bias that causes people to be more sensitive to prospective losses than gains. Loss aversion can cause investors to be too cautious and steer clear of riskier investments that could yield better returns. Investors can make more educated and logical decisions about their risk tolerance and investment strategy by being aware of their psychological biases and tendencies.

In conclusion, we all face daily risks, whether traveling to work, surfing a 60-foot wave, making investments, or running a business. Risk is the likelihood that an investment won't perform as well as you'd want or lose money. In the financial sector, the risk is the probability that an investment's actual return will differ from anticipated.

Regular risk assessment and diversification are the most effective ways to control investing risk. Diversification can increase returns based on your goals and target degree of risk, even while it won't ensure gains or protect against losses. Investors and business managers can achieve their financial goals by making investments they are most comfortable with by finding the correct balance between risk and return.

Conclusion

The easiest way to get started is to start once you've decided on your financial goals and where you want to invest. To build up your confidence to invest more money over the long run, you might wish to test out your selected platform with a smaller sum first.

There is no specific period when you should hold your investments when it comes to investing, but we advise keeping them for at least five years to even out the ups and downs. Your financial goals should determine the length of your investment. For instance, if you are 35 and want to retire at age 55, you must invest for at least 20 years.

As with any investment, you should only invest if you are prepared to put your money down for a few years while being aware that there is a chance you could lose money or make money. You mustn't immediately spend any money you might need, like your emergency cash reserves.